CINDY WOODEN

PAUL HARING

POPE FRANCIS
A GUIDE TO GOD'S TIME

Catholic News Service

LIBRERIA EDITRICE VATICANA

Libreria Editrice Vaticana
00120 Città del Vaticano
Tel. (+39) 06.698.81032 – Fax (+39) 06.698.84716
www.libreriaeditricevaticana.va
www.vatican.va

Catholic News Service/U.S. Conference of Catholic Bishops
3211 Fourth St. N.E.
Washington, D.C. 20017
Tel. (+1) 202 541-3279 – Fax (+1) 202 541-3117
www.catholicnews.com
www.usccb.org

ISBN 978-1-60137-498-1

COVER: BALCONY OF ST. PETER'S BASILICA, DEC. 25, 2013

CONTENTS

Entering God's Time

"The liturgy is God's time and God's space," Pope Francis said in a homily early one winter morning during a Mass at his Vatican residence. "We put ourselves there in God's time and space, and we don't look at our watches."

Pope Francis: A Guide to God's Time invites you to enter God's time and space by joining Pope Francis for a journey through the church's year of worship – the liturgical year. Our journey with the pope extends from the seasons of Advent and Christmas to the familiar weeks of Ordinary Time. It moves from Lent and the days of the Triduum (Holy Thursday, Good Friday and Easter), to Easter Time and back again to Ordinary Time. As Pope Francis leads us through the liturgical year, we also will pause with him to celebrate special feasts of the Blessed Virgin Mary – the premier disciple – and to contemplate over and over again God's love for us, his mercy and his call for us to become merciful in turn.

BALCONY OF ST. PETER'S BASILICA, **MARCH 13, 2013**

Even if a large part of the calendar year is labeled *Ordinary Time* by the church, its year of worship is never ordinary! It is extraordinary at every point both in its celebration of God's goodness and mercy, and in all it reveals about God's dynamic presence in our daily lives. In the pages that follow, Pope Francis affirms again and again that the liturgical year addresses us directly, both as communities and as individuals and families.

The rhythm of every Mass and the focus of its prayers and readings are meant to help Catholics step away from their busy lives and enter into God's time. Pope Francis suggests to worshipers that with the Mass and the liturgical year, Catholics do not transform time, God does.

Pope Francis celebrates the Mass each day of the liturgical year with either a large Mass at St. Peter's Basilica or in a parish church, or with a more intimate early-morning Mass in the Holy Spirit Chapel of the Do-

ST. PETER'S SQUARE, MARCH 19, 2013

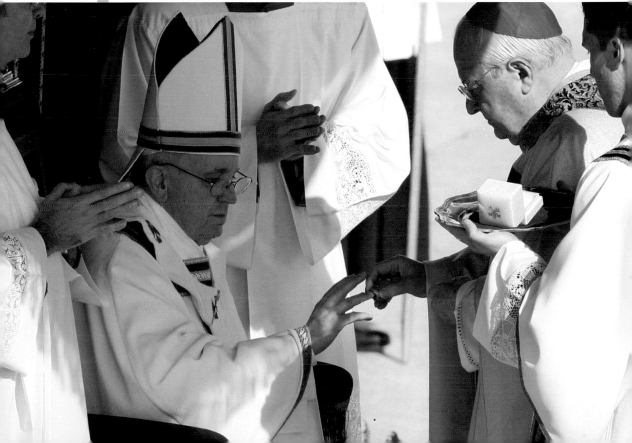

mus Sanctae Marthae. The *domus* is the Vatican guesthouse where he and the other cardinals stayed during the conclave that elected him pope. After his election March 13, 2013, Pope Francis astonished many with his decision to continue living there.

Rather than celebrate with just his closest assistants, as many popes did before him, Pope Francis invites a small group – usually about 80 people – to pray with and for him. The first invitations to participate in the morning Mass with Pope Francis went to the most humble of Vatican employees: the gardeners and garbage collectors. The guesthouse cooks and cleaning crews participated in the Mass another day. Employees from the offices of the Roman Curia, Vatican Radio and even a group of journalists and photographers who regularly cover Vatican events are just some of the many others invited to these Masses.

St. Peter's Basilica, Feb. 22, 2014

While the modern chapel in the Domus Sanctae Marthae is decorated with a few bunches of flowers, which themselves reflect the season of the year, the movement through the church's liturgical year is signaled more visibly by the color of vestments the pope and other priest concelebrants wear (green in Ordinary Time, for example, purple during Advent and Lent, red on martyrs' feast days). Very notably, the pope's homilies, reflecting on the Scripture readings of each Mass, bring the liturgical seasons into clear view.

Pope Francis attaches great importance to homilies. That is clear from the lengthy space he devotes to preaching in "The Joy of the Gospel" (*Evangelii Gaudium*), a major document called an apostolic exhortation published Nov. 24, 2013. In it Pope Francis advises preachers on preparing and delivering homilies, insisting that the priority must be to help people change their lives. He encourages the homilist "to keep his ear to the people" in order to know their needs.

"In some people we see an ostentatious preoccupation for the liturgy, for doctrine and for the church's prestige, but without any concern that the Gospel have a real impact on God's faithful people and the concrete needs of the present time," he states in the apostolic exhortation. On the other hand, he writes, it is possible to be so concerned about questions of politics, social justice and the congregation's daily lives that the Mass betrays a "spiritual worldliness" on the part of participants or turns into a "self-help" session.

ST. ANNE'S PARISH, VATICAN, MARCH 17, 2013

The pope's homilies at the morning Mass in the Domus Sanctae Marthae are not scripted fully in advance but are prepared with prayer. Pope Francis begins each day by rising around 4:30 a.m. and opening his extremely well-worn breviary, a prayer book containing the Liturgy of the Hours. As that title suggests, the prayer book is another way of helping Catholics sanctify time and dedicate their day, their week and their seasons to God.

Morning Prayer, selections from the writings of the fathers and doctors of the church, Evening Prayer and Night Prayer are main components of the Liturgy of the Hours. Its psalms, readings and prayer texts change not only with the liturgical season but also with the time of day.

Sensitive to the rhythms of real life, Morning Prayer helps people dedicate the day ahead to the Lord. With Night Prayer they look back at what they did or failed to do during the day now drawing to a close.

14

Pope Francis also continues a practice at the Domus Sanctae Marthae that he began long ago in Argentina, his homeland: He spends one hour in the evening – usually 7 to 8 p.m. – in silent adoration before the Eucharist.

When he tells people about this hour of adoration, he is very realistic. He acknowledges that people sometimes might doze off, as he does occasionally. In "adoring Christ truly present in the Eucharist," he urges Catholics to recognize who they are, then offer that to Christ and allow him to transform them.

Two things stand out about Pope Francis when he celebrates the Eucharist, whether at daily Mass in the Domus Sanctae Marthae or at more solemn celebrations in the grandeur of St. Peter's Basilica: a striking preference for simplicity of vestments and furnishings, and homilies closely tied to the day's Scripture readings and the lives of ordinary Catholics.

As the liturgical year leads people step by step into Jesus' ministry, passion, death and resurrection, Pope Francis reflects on events in the Lord's life and what they reveal about God's great love for people and mercy toward those who stray. But the pope also includes practical advice for Christians about following Jesus by extending love and mercy in concrete ways to all, especially the poor and to those living on society's margins.

The pope's messages run the gamut from urging people to give up gossiping and speaking ill of others to ensuring that when they give to people begging money, they look them in the eye, smile and always treat them with dignity, recognizing in their faces the face of Christ.

ST. PETER'S BASILICA, FEB. 22, 2014

THE LITURGICAL YEAR

Though it often feels that one day of the week or year is much like all the others, people tend naturally to mark time in a variety of ways. We look forward to (or dread) the changing of seasons, and we prepare for that change in ways big and small. We also personalize our year with special celebrations of anniversaries and birthdays, marking significant dates on our calendars, even in the lives of loved ones who perhaps died years ago.

Pope Francis and the entire Christian community do the same thing. The term *liturgical year* refers to the church's way of marking time, setting aside some weeks for preparation and others for special celebration.

Even the weeks of Ordinary Time are punctuated by remembering special events in the life of Jesus, his mother, Mary, and the saints. Ordi-

ST. THOMAS THE APOSTLE PARISH, ROME, FEB. 16, 2014

nary Time appears twice a year on the church's calendar, lasting from just after the feast of the Baptism of the Lord until Ash Wednesday and from the day after Pentecost until Advent begins.

On the church's Latin-rite calendar, the first Sunday of Advent signals the start of a new year. Everything begins again as the prayers and readings at Mass remind Christians of the need to change their lives not only in preparation for the coming celebration of Jesus' birth, but in anticipation of his second coming too.

Advent is the time of preparation for Christmas and the Christmas season, which begins with Mass the evening of Dec. 24. The 12 days of Christmas, made famous in the traditional holiday song, conclude with the arrival of Epiphany, traditionally celebrated Jan. 6, although many Catholics now observe Epiphany the Sunday between Jan. 2 and 8. However, Christmas Time does not end there.

St. Anne's Parish, Vatican, **March 17, 2013**

Epiphany recalls the visit of the three Wise Men from the East to Jesus, the Messiah. Pope Francis said on Epiphany 2014 that "the destiny of every person is symbolized in this journey of the Magi of the East: Our life is a journey" that should lead to Christ. With the three kings coming from a foreign land, Epiphany also proclaims that the mission of Christ addresses all peoples.

Christmas draws to a close on the liturgical calendar with the feast of the Baptism of the Lord when Jesus rises from the baptismal waters and a voice from heaven says, "This is my beloved Son, with whom I am well pleased" (Mt 3:17).

The earliest Christian communities accorded unique importance to one very special event – not the birth of Jesus but his resurrection. Easter for them became the Sunday of Sundays when they celebrated the Lord's resurrection from the dead and the start of a new creation.

During a special period before Easter that we know as Lent, they carefully prepared candidates for baptism on that key day. The rest of the community members readied themselves during this season to renew their own baptismal promises at Easter.

While Lent is a time of prayer, almsgiving and fasting that now lasts

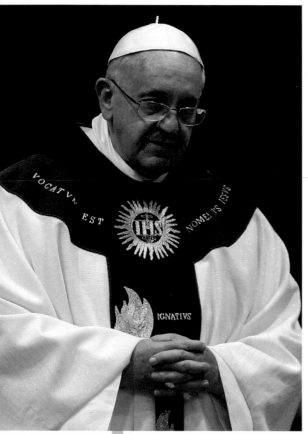

some 40 days (not counting its Sundays), the Easter season prolongs the feasting of the great day, stretching over the 50 days to Pentecost.

After Pentecost, commemorating the Holy Spirit's descent on the apostles and their being sent into the world to continue Jesus' ministry, it is back to Ordinary Time. Now the Scripture readings at Mass focus on Jesus' ministry, his preaching and parables.

However, as the year draws on and the days start getting shorter in the Northern Hemisphere, the Ordinary Time readings look more and more toward the end of the world and God's promise that Christ the King will conquer death and renew the world. One liturgical year ends and another begins with the first Sunday of Advent and the preparations for commemorating Christ's birth.

CHURCH OF THE GESÙ, ROME, JAN. 3, 2014

ST. PETER'S SQUARE, DEC. 5, 2013

"ADVENT IS A TIME

OF WAITING

FOR THE LORD. ...

THE LORD IS COMING!

LET US WAIT FOR HIM!"

(POPE FRANCIS, ADVENT 2013)

Advent's first Sunday signals the start of a new liturgical year, "a new journey of the people of God with Jesus Christ, our Shepherd, who guides us through history toward the fulfillment of the kingdom of God," Pope Francis said as Advent began in 2013.

Therefore, this Sunday possesses a "special charm," he explained. "It makes us experience deeply the meaning of history. We rediscover the beauty of all being on a journey: the church, with her vocation and mission, and all humanity, peoples, civilizations, cultures, all on a journey across the paths of time."

As Catholics light one candle after another on their Advent wreaths, the church's prayer prepares them again to encounter and adore Jesus, the Word made flesh, born in a manger to offer humanity hope and assure us that God's promises will be fulfilled. In Advent the church also

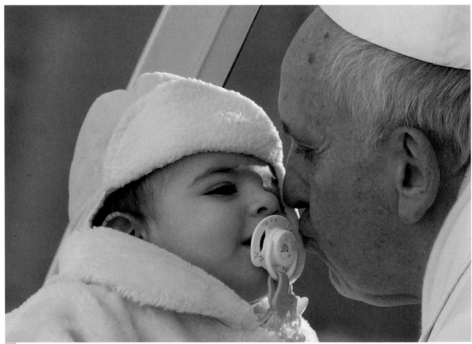

St. Peter's Square, Dec. 18, 2013

looks forward to Christ's second coming, his promise to come again in glory at the end of time.

During the weeks of Advent, Christians await the coming of the Lord with a sense of expectation and delight. "The journey of life is precisely this: journeying in order to meet Jesus," Pope Francis said when he visited a Rome parish Dec. 1, 2013.

Christians also ready themselves during Advent to celebrate the Lord's coming. So like Lent, the other major season of preparation on the church's calendar, Advent includes a penitential element. This is a season of conversion and renewal, and a time to clean house, as it were. The biblical readings for the Advent Sundays begin with a wakeup call: "Be watchful! Be alert! You do not know when the time will come" (Mk 13:33) or "At an hour you do not expect, the Son of Man will come" (Mt 24:44).

BALDACCHINO, St. Peter's Basilica, Dec. 18, 2012

Early in Advent, on the Dec. 8 feast of the Immaculate Conception, Catholics celebrate God's decision to redeem the Virgin Mary "from the moment of her conception," preserving her from original sin (Catechism of the Catholic Church, 491). On this day in 2013, Pope Francis described Mary as a simple young woman from a small town in the countryside; she is blessed by God, yet must still respond yes to God's plan for her life. But the pope cautioned against thinking that "the mystery of this girl from Nazareth" is "estranged from us." Instead, "we are connected. Indeed, God rests his loving gaze on every man and every woman!"

Mary, the pope said, "teaches us how to live this Advent season in expectation of the Lord. For this time of Advent is a time of waiting for the Lord." The pope exclaimed: "The Lord is coming! Let us wait for him!"

When people grow weary and feel the weight of sinfulness or when they struggle to keep moving forward with hope in the new life Christ brings, Pope Francis wants them to realize how strongly the Scripture readings for Advent Masses emphasize God's love, tenderness and forgiveness. In fact, he wants people to know that the strength to recognize their sins and ask God's mercy comes from knowing that God will welcome them back with open arms. "The Lord, the great God, is not afraid of tenderness. He is tenderness, he

BALDACCHINO, ST. PETER'S BASILICA, DEC. 18, 2012

is born a baby, he makes himself small," the pope insisted during a Mass one Advent day in the chapel at the Domus Sanctae Marthae, his Vatican residence.

A desperate search for the perfect gift to give someone may be part of many people's Advent days, but Pope Francis thinks it might be even tougher to find the perfect Advent atmosphere: a bit of silence. It is good

during this season to listen to God, who speaks quietly, tenderly, like a mother or father, the pope stressed in another early-morning Advent homily. "When a child has a bad dream and wakes up crying, Dad goes and says: 'Don't be afraid, don't be scared. I'm here.' The Lord speaks this way too."

That, said the pope, "is the music of the language of the Lord, and we, in preparation for Christmas, ought to hear it." While Christmas usually "seems to be a very noisy holiday," he was confident "it would do us good to have a little silence and to hear these words of love, these words of such nearness, these words of tenderness."

SPANISH STEPS, ROME, DEC. 8, 2013

GAUDETE SUNDAY

Advent's third Sunday is different from the others and enjoys a special name, *Gaudete* or *Rejoice* Sunday. "In the liturgy the invitation rings out several times to rejoice. Why? Because the Lord is near. Christmas is near," Pope Francis explained on this day in 2013. Many Catholics light a pink candle on their Advent wreaths, and priests may wear rose-colored vestments.

This day's joy comes from knowing that God loves you, will help you and will save you. Thanks to God's help, "we can always begin again," Pope Francis made clear. He acknowledged that someone might say: "No, Father, I did so many reprehensible things; I am a great sinner. I cannot begin from scratch!" But the pope stated emphatically: "You can begin from scratch" because God "is waiting for you, he is close to you, he loves you, he is merciful, he forgives you, he gives you the strength to begin again from scratch! Everybody!"

As a result, "we are able to open our eyes again, to overcome sadness" and "to strike up a new song," Pope Francis told a crowd gathered in St. Peter's Square. This is "true joy," he said, and it "remains even amid trial, even amid suffering, for it is not a superficial joy because it permeates the depths of the person who entrusts himself to the Lord and confides in him."

MARY AND JOSEPH

As Advent drew to a close in 2013, Pope Francis asked Catholics to imagine themselves as Mary. During Advent's final week "the church is like Mary: She is awaiting a birth," Pope Francis said. Like Mary, believers should say to Jesus and mean with all their hearts: "Come! I want to see your face."

The church of Advent keeps watch as Mary did, the pope told participants in a Mass at his residence. Watching, he said, "is the virtue, the attitude, of pilgrims." He asked in his homily: "Are we watching or are we closed? Are we vigilant or are we safe and secure in an inn and we no longer want to continue on? Are we pilgrims or are we wandering?"

Pope Francis also spoke during Advent's final days about St. Joseph and the dilemma he faced. Joseph was a good, God-fearing man who fol-

MANGER SQUARE, BETHLEHEM, MAY 25, 2014

lowed the laws and customs of his people. He "always listened to the voice of God," the pope observed. According to the customs of his people, he should have sent Mary away when he found before they were married that she was expecting a child. But God sent an angel to Joseph in a dream to tell him the child was conceived through the power of the Holy Spirit.

Joseph "was following a good plan for his life, but God was reserving another plan for him, a greater mission," Pope Francis noted. He described Joseph as a man "deeply sensitive" to God's will, "a man attentive to the messages that came to him from the depths of his heart and from on high." So Joseph "did not persist in following his own plan for his life, he did not allow bitterness to poison his soul; rather, he was ready to make himself available to the news that, in a such a bewildering way, was being presented to him."

St. Peter's Square, **Dec. 15, 2013**

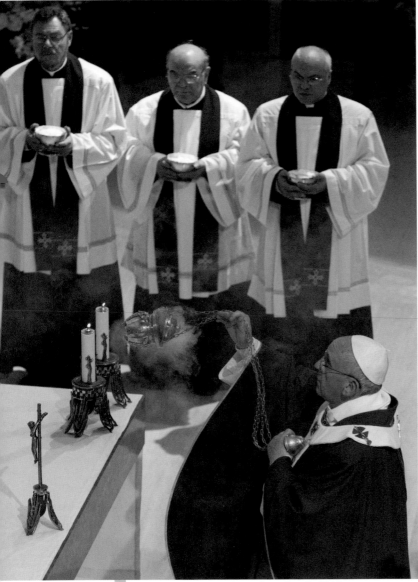

Pope Francis presented Mary and Joseph as models to follow during the last days of Advent, when Christmas rapidly approaches. In remarks for the Sunday Angelus just three days before Christmas, he exhorted Christians to "walk together toward Bethlehem" with Mary, "the woman full of grace who had the courage to entrust herself totally to the Word of God," and with Joseph, "the faithful and just man who chose to believe the Lord rather than listen to the voices of doubt and human pride."

ST. PETER'S SQUARE, DEC. 24, 2013

Tidings of Christmas

"Looking

at the child

in the manger,

child of peace,

our thoughts turn

to those children

who are the most

vulnerable

victims of wars,

but we think too

of the elderly,

battered women,

the sick."

(Pope FRANCIS, Christmas 2013)

"This is the message of Christmas: The Word became flesh." Christmas thus reveals "the immense love that God has for humanity." That was Pope Francis' repeated observation during his pontificate's first Christmas season. Christmas means that God "loves us" and "walks with us."

On the church's calendar, Christmas begins in the evening darkness of Dec. 24 with the proclamation that "a Savior has been born for you" (Lk 2:11). The season's celebration continues through January's feast of the Baptism of the Lord.

"God willed to share in our human condition to the point of becoming one with us in the person of Jesus," Pope Francis explained as Christmas 2013 drew near. But God's presence "did not take place in a perfect, idyllic world, but rather in this real world, which is marked by so many things both good and bad, by division, wickedness, poverty, arrogance

St. Alphonsus Liguori Parish, Rome, Jan. 6, 2014

and war." In this way, the pope continued, God "demonstrated in an un-equaled manner his merciful and truly loving disposition toward the human creature. He is God-with-us."

For Pope Francis, to think of Christmas only as a sweet feast cele-brating the birth of a perfectly plump baby in a warm, cozy manger is to miss what truly is astounding about Jesus' birth. The Incarnation shows how much God loves us, and it moves believers to love and care for each other. Since that very first Christmas, it is clear that God is "to be found where man passes his days in joy or in sorrow." Thus, Pope Francis said, our world "is no longer only 'a valley of tears'" but "the place where God himself has pitched his tent; it is the meeting place of God with man."

These considerations bear important implications for believers' lives. Pope Francis pointed out that "if God, in the Christmas mystery, reveals himself not as one who remains on high and dominates the uni-

ST. PETER'S SQUARE, DEC. 31, 2013

verse, but as the one who bends down, descends to the little and poor earth, it means that, to be like him, we should not put ourselves above others, but indeed lower ourselves, place ourselves at the service of others, become small with the small and poor with the poor."

Christian life is a journey. In his first homily as pope – delivered March 14, 2013, to the cardinals who had elected him the evening before – Pope Francis shared his conviction that following Christ involves setting out and walking on. "Our life is a journey, and when we stop moving, things go wrong," he said to the cardinals.

But during the journey of Christian life we are not alone. Pope Francis told participants in the 2013 Christmas Midnight Mass in St. Peter's Basilica that Jesus "has entered our history, he has shared our journey." And who is Jesus? He is "love incarnate." Jesus "is not simply a teacher of wisdom" nor is he "an ideal for which we strive while know-

ST. PETER'S BASILICA, DEC. 24, 2013

ST. PETER'S BASILICA, DEC. 24, 2013

ing we are hopelessly distant from it. He is the meaning of life and history, who has pitched his tent in our midst."

At noon Christmas Day, St. Peter's Square fills to overflowing with pilgrims, tourists, families, Swiss Guards, the Vatican police band and Italian military squadrons. All eyes are on the central balcony of St. Peter's Basilica where the pope solemnly will offer his blessing *urbi et orbi* ("to the city and the world"). Celebrating the birth of the Prince of Peace, the pope pleads for universal solidarity and peace.

"I take up the song of the angels who appeared to the shepherds in Bethlehem the night Jesus was born," Pope Francis said in his 2013 Christmas midday message. "It is a song that unites heaven and earth, giving praise and glory to heaven, and the promise of peace" on earth. This song is "for every man or woman who keeps watch through the night, who hopes for a better world, who cares for others while humbly seeking to do his or her duty."

One day after Christmas the church celebrates the feast of St. Stephen, the first Christian martyr. Speaking in St. Peter's Square on this feast day, Pope Francis recalled how St. Stephen – presented in the Acts of the Apostles as "a man full of faith and of the Holy Spirit" (6:5), who served widows and the poor – was dragged outside Jerusalem's walls and stoned to death after a "fiery dispute" led to him being accused of blas-

St. Peter's Basilica, Dec. 24, 2013

phemy before the Sanhedrin, a Jewish court. Stephen, Pope Francis noted, died "like Jesus, asking pardon for those who killed him."

The Dec. 26 feast appears to contrast jarringly with the festivities of Christmas. So Pope Francis asked, "Why disturb the charm with the memory of such atrocious violence?" In reality, the pope replied, "today we celebrate the 'birth' of Stephen, which in its depths springs from the birth of Christ. Jesus transforms the death of those who love him into a dawn of new life!" The feast of Stephen "dispels a false image of Christmas: the fairy-tale, sugarcoated image, which is not in the Gospel," Pope Francis said. It reminds us that salvation passes "through

the narrow door of the cross."

The Christmas season also reminds us that the Lord was born into a human family. Celebrating the feast of the Holy Family the Sunday after Christmas, Pope Francis did not sugarcoat or turn away from the realities of life for Mary, Joseph and the newborn Jesus. Focusing on their flight into Egypt, which made them "refugees," the pope urged concern for everyone forced to flee their homeland. "Jesus wanted to belong to a family who experienced these hardships so that no one would feel excluded from the loving closeness of God," the pope said. "The flight into Egypt caused by Herod's threat shows us that God is present where man is in danger, where man is suffering, where he is fleeing, where he experiences rejection." But God is present too "where man dreams," hoping "to return in freedom to his homeland" and looking ahead to "life for his family and dignity for himself and his loved ones."

EPIPHANY

With the arrival of the great feast of Epiphany, the church again focuses upon a journey, the journey of the Magi – the three kings or Wise Men from the East who follow a star leading them to Jesus. Thus, on Epiphany Catholics celebrate the revelation of Jesus to "the nations." Speaking on Epiphany 2014, Pope Francis noted that "because Jesus came for us all, for every nation, for everyone," the liturgy now acclaims, "Lord, every nation on earth will adore you."

Often Pope Francis emphasizes that human beings must set off, leave their old ways behind and actively search for the Lord, but he insists the initiative in this always is God's. Speaking Jan. 6,

St. Peter's Square, Jan. 6, 2014

2014, in St. Peter's Square, Pope Francis described the star the Magi followed as "a sign of the birth of Christ," a sign God set in the sky for them. He said, "Had they not seen the star, these men would not have set out." God's grace "precedes us," the pope stressed, "and this grace appeared in Jesus. He is the Epiphany. He, Jesus Christ, is the manifestation of God's love."

THE BAPTISM OF THE LORD

Christmas Time for the popes draws to its close with the sounds of trickling water and crying babies under Michelangelo's magnificently frescoed Sistine Chapel ceiling. The chapel is the site for the pope's an-

BETHANY BEYOND THE JORDAN, MAY 24, 2013

nual celebration of the feast of the Baptism of the Lord. During a Mass, the pope baptizes numerous infants, mostly sons and daughters of Vatican employees and Swiss Guards.

After his first experience of this tradition, Pope Francis told people gathered in St. Peter's Square: "This morning I baptized 32 infants. With you I thank the Lord for these creatures and for every new life. I am glad to baptize babies. I like it very much! Every newborn child is a gift of joy and hope, and each baby that is baptized is a miracle of faith and a celebration for the family of God."

Then the pope offered a few concluding comments on Christmas to the gathering, explaining that if God remained closed off in heaven, human life on earth would be dark and without hope. But in the Christmas season, "once again faith has given us the certainty that the heavens have been rent with the coming of Christ. And on the day of the baptism of Christ we continue to contemplate the heavens opened. The manifestation of the Son of God on earth marks the beginning of the great time of mercy," because

BALCONY OF ST. PETER'S BASILICA, DEC. 25, 2013

"God gives us in Christ the guarantee of an indestructible love" and the ability to become God's sons and daughters.

SISTINE CHAPEL, VATICAN, JAN. 12, 2014

ST. PETER'S SQUARE, APRIL 13, 2014

Hearts in Lent

"With its invitations to conversion, Lent comes providentially to awaken us, to rouse us from torpor, from the risk of moving forward by inertia."

(Pope FRANCIS, Ash Wednesday 2014)

ent "is a 'powerful' season." It is "a turning point that can foster change and conversion in each of us," Pope Francis told the people gathered in St. Peter's Square on Ash Wednesday 2014. Speaking during his weekly general audience, he explained that "the church issues two important invitations" during Lent. The first is to develop "greater awareness of the redemptive work of Christ." The second is "to live out one's baptism with deeper commitment." Pope Francis said, "We all need to improve, to change for the better." Lent helps us to leave behind "old habits" and a "lazy addiction to the evil that deceives and ensnares us."

The Lenten weeks are set aside for increased prayer, charitable giving and fasting in preparation for Easter, the great feast of salvation. Connecting the notion of growth with movement, as he almost always does, Pope Francis described Lent in an Ash Wednesday homily as "a

BASILICA OF SANTA SABINA, ROME, MARCH 5, 2014

journey on which, by defying routine, we strive to open our eyes and ears, but especially to open our hearts, in order to go beyond our own back yard." Thus, his Lent is not solely about interior contemplation, self-control and will power, but about recognizing God in those who suffer and learning to respond to them as Jesus would.

The Gospel reading for Lent's first Sunday describes Jesus going into the desert, fasting 40 days and being tempted by the devil. "The tempter seeks to divert Jesus from the Father's plan, that is, from the way of sacrifice, of the love that offers itself in expiation, to make him take an easier path, one of success and power," but Jesus "decisively rejects" these temptations, Pope Francis observed as Lent began in 2014. Jesus responds by turning to God's word and quoting biblical passages back to Satan. "Jesus is well aware that there can be no dialogue with Satan, for he is cunning," the pope stated. That is why, rather than "engag-

ST. PETER'S BASILICA, MARCH 28, 2014

ing in dialogue" with Satan, Jesus chooses "to take refuge in the word of God and responds with the power of this word." Today's Christians should respond similarly to temptation, the pope exhorted his listeners, saying that at the moment of temptation "there is no arguing with Satan," so "our defense must always be the word of God!"

Satan, for Pope Francis, is not a figure of mythology or human invention. It is not "old-fashioned" to speak of the devil today, the pope remarked one morning during a Lenten Mass in the chapel of his Vatican residence. "The devil exists even in the 21st century, and we must not be naive," he said. "We must learn from the Gospel how to battle against him."

Again and again in Lent 2014 Pope Francis urged people to read the Bible. Then he had an idea: To make the point more concretely, give people a copy of the Gospels. Seminarians, nuns and Scouts handed out thousands of copies of a pocket-sized edition of the Gospels in St. Peter's Square April 6, Lent's fifth Sunday. Later that day, the Gospels were distributed when Pope Francis visited Rome's St. Gregory The Great Church. "I would like to give you the Gospel, which you can take home," he announced to parishioners. Then, during Holy Week, a papal envoy distributed more than 1,000 copies of the Gospels to inmates at Rome's Regina Coeli prison.

The small paperback format of the Gospels was chosen to make it easy to carry around so people might read it while waiting in line or riding the bus. But another

St. Gregory the Great Parish, Rome, April 6, 2014

St. Peter's Square, March 24, 2013

option the pope proposed was to download a Bible app to "a smartphone or tablet." He said, "The important thing is to read the word of God" by some means because "it is Jesus who is speaking there."

Listening to Jesus also was the point highlighted the second Sunday of Lent 2014 when the Gospel reading was the famous account of the Transfiguration. We hear how Jesus goes up a high mountain with Peter, James and John and is transfigured before their eyes; his face shines, and his clothes turn dazzling white. "This is my beloved Son, … listen to him" (Mt 17:5), a voice from heaven calls. The heart of Lent's call for Pope Francis is to listen to Jesus. "We, the disciples of Jesus, are called to be people who listen to his voice and take his words seriously," the pope emphasized. However, "to listen to Jesus, we must be close to him."

Pope Francis acknowledged that, like the first disciples, everyone sometimes needs to follow Jesus up a mountain and remain there with him quietly, peacefully. "This we do in prayer." But, he cautioned, "we cannot stay" on the mountain. "An encounter with God in prayer inspires us anew to 'descend the mountain' and return to the plain where we meet many brothers and sisters weighed down by fatigue, sickness, injustice, ignorance and poverty – both material and spiritual." We then

Copacabana beach, Rio de Janeiro, Brazil, July 27, 2013

are called "to bear the fruit of that experience with God by sharing the grace we have received."

St. Peter's Basilica, March 28, 2014

52

SACRAMENT OF RECONCILIATION

For Pope Francis the Lenten journey includes the sacrament of penance, or reconciliation. He recommends regular practice of this sacrament year round, once informing us that "even the pope confesses every two weeks because the pope is also a sinner." On monthly visits to Rome parishes, he arrives early so he can meet special parish groups and hear several confessions. But during Lent 2014 he wanted to give more people an opportunity to experience the sacrament's healing, so he scheduled a public penance service in St. Peter's Basilica. An army of priests stood by in dozens of confessionals or sat on plastic chairs in quiet nooks of the massive church. One confessional was set aside for the pope to hear confessions. But first, en route to his assigned spot, he suddenly turned and knelt before a priest to confess and receive absolution himself.

It is not enough, though, to get several hundred people to participate in the sacrament of reconciliation. Pope Francis wants them to share with others the sense of joy that comes with forgiveness. During the penance service he remarked: "If you go to [the Father] with your whole life, even with many sins, instead of reproaching you, he will rejoice. ... This is something you must tell others today."

If sharing the Good News with others tops the pope's to-do list, gossiping seems to top his list of actions to avoid. He speaks often about the "poison" of gossip, one of the devil's favorite seductions. It begins as a "dark pleasure," spreads and is all too easy to justify. "We are all tempted to gossip. Well, maybe one of you is a saint and is not tempted, but I have been tempted to gossip. It's a daily temptation," he said in a homily one Lenten morning. Nearly a year earlier, soon after his March 2013 election, he tied gossip to one of Lent's more dramatic moments, when Judas

St. Peter's Square, April 13, 2014

54

betrays Jesus for 30 pieces of silver. Pope Francis characterized gossip as "a form of selling," since it treats someone like "merchandise." When we gossip about someone, he said, we do "the same thing Judas did."

Those who participated in the Lenten reconciliation service with Pope Francis heard him describe how good behavior flows "from the heart of the person renewed in the likeness of God." It is a matter of clothing oneself with "new attitudes" that lead to speaking the truth and avoiding "all deceit," and to sharing "all you have with others, especially those in need." Moreover, a person renewed in God's likeness does not "give in to anger, resentment and revenge," but is "ready to forgive" and to look for everyone's "good side."

The call to repentance and conversion "introduces us to two essential elements of Christian life," Pope Francis explained. In

HOLY STAIRS, ROME, MARCH 10, 2014

addition to the invitation to put on "a new nature," Christians are called to abide in love – to love others as God loves them. And love, he stressed, "is open, it spreads and bears fruit, it always kindles new love."

COLOSSEUM, ROME, MARCH 29, 2013

AND DEATH TO RESURRECTION

"THE MOMENT
OF SUFFERING,
WHEN MANY PEOPLE
FEEL THE NEED
TO GET DOWN
FROM THE CROSS,
IS THE MOMENT
CLOSEST
TO THE RESURRECTION.
NIGHT BECOMES
DARKEST JUST BEFORE
MORNING DAWNS."

(POPE FRANCIS, APRIL 16, 2014)

n the deep darkness of Good Friday night in 2013, Rome's Colosseum was lit by torches as tens of thousands of people gathered quietly with prayer booklets and candles. Pope Francis said to them: "Sometimes it seems God doesn't respond to evil, that he keeps silent. But in reality God has spoken, he has responded. His response is the cross of Christ: a word that is love, mercy, forgiveness."

The pope then invited the crowd to "walk together along the Way of the Cross" and to go "forward, waiting for the resurrection of Jesus, who loves us so much." For the church, the life-giving mystery of Christ's passion and death points toward his resurrection.

Good Friday in Holy Week arrives during the intense period of prayer and celebration known as the Sacred Paschal Triduum, spanning the period from Holy Thursday to Easter. The Triduum stands at the

RIO DE JANEIRO, BRAZIL, JULY 26, 2013

heart of the liturgical year. In fact, throughout the year the liturgy reflects the Triduum's message of suffering, death and new life.

The Triduum, which literally means "three days," is the culmination of Holy Week. This is the week Pope Francis described as an opportunity to relive "the crowning moment" of Jesus' earthly journey and of the "plan of love that runs through the entire history of relations between God and humanity."

The Triduum begins on Holy Thursday with the Mass of the Lord's Supper, celebrating the institution of the Eucharist and the priesthood. This day is followed by the meditative Liturgy of the Lord's Passion on Good Friday. Finally, Easter arrives. In the glow of candlelit churches, the Easter Vigil Mass announces the Lord's resurrection.

"In the Triduum of the passion, death and resurrection of Jesus, human suffering is taken up completely and redeemed by God, by the God

ST. PETER'S BASILICA, APRIL 17, 2014

who is love. Only Christ gives meaning to the scandal of the suffering of the innocent," Pope Francis said in April 2014 to a group of physicians who deal daily with cancer patients of all ages.

Just before the Triduum began in 2013, Pope Francis held his first-ever weekly general audience, addressing a crowd of about 15,000 people in St. Peter's Square. He asked them to move out of their comfort zones in order to bring God's love and mercy to others.

"Living Holy Week means entering ever more deeply into the logic of God, into the logic of the cross, which is not primarily that of suffering and death, but rather that of love and of the gift of self which brings life. It means entering into the logic of the Gospel," said the pope. He stressed that "following and accompanying Christ" requires that we "come out of ourselves, out of a dreary way of living the faith that has become a habit, out of the temptation to withdraw into our

St. Peter's Basilica, April 17, 2014

own plans, which end up shutting out God's creative action." We are called, Pope Francis insisted, "to come out" into the world "and to do so with God's love and tenderness, with respect and with patience, knowing that God takes our hands, our feet, our heart, and guides them."

At Pope Francis' general audience in St. Peter's Square one year

CENACLE, JERUSALEM, MAY 26, 2014

later, he again suggested ways for pilgrims to approach the Triduum, proposing a practical task: "Look at the crucifix," he said. Dying on the cross was "the worst form of death, reserved for slaves and criminals." Yet, the pope pointed out, Jesus willingly accepted that death to show the depth of his love. For, "God intervenes with the power of his resur-

rection" in the moments "when all seems lost, when no one remains" and when "hope is shattered."

Pope Francis counseled his listeners that the moments when "we fail to find any way out of our difficulties, when we sink in the thickest darkness," are the very moments when "we experience that we are frail and are sinners." However, it is then "that we must not deny our failure but rather open ourselves trustingly to hope in God, as Jesus did."

Holy Week is a time "to think deeply about the suffering of Jesus," the pope said. "Let us say to ourselves: This is for my sake. Even if I had been the only person in the world, he would have done it. He did it for me."

By tradition, the pope does not preach at the Good Friday Liturgy of the Lord's Passion in St. Peter's Basilica, but he usually makes a few remarks late that night after the Way of the Cross service at Rome's Colosseum. At the 2014 service, Pope Francis said that looking upon the cross, Christians see the full weight of sin, betrayal and selfishness, "the monstrosity of humanity when it lets itself be guided by

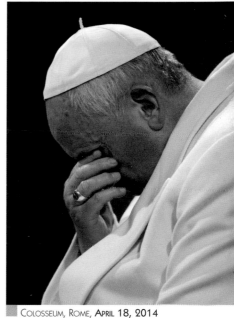

COLOSSEUM, ROME, APRIL 18, 2014

evil." Yet, the cross is the instrument of salvation; it demonstrates "the immensity of the mercy of God." The pope prayerfully pleaded, "Jesus, guide us from the cross to the resurrection, and teach us that evil shall not have the last word, but love, mercy and forgiveness will."

ST. PETER'S BASILICA, APRIL 18, 2014

YOUR "ROLE" IN THE GOSPEL

Preparing Catholics for Holy Week and the Triduum in 2014, Pope Francis proposed a meditation similar in style to what he learned as a Jesuit from the Spiritual Exercises of St. Ignatius of Loyola, founder of the Society of Jesus. This method of prayer suggests that people imagine themselves as a character in a biblical scene. They might describe a biblical story's setting or ask how its characters interact or react to Jesus. Praying with Scripture in this way, a person could ask: Which character in this story am I? As that character, what are my thoughts and feelings?

Pope Francis, addressing a crowd mainly of young people present for his Palm Sunday celebration in St. Peter's Square, set aside his prepared homily and encouraged them to enter the Gospel stories of the Lord's passion and death, and ask, "Who am I before my Lord?"

The pope challenged the young people to ask themselves: "Am I like Judas," who betrays Jesus for 30 pieces of silver? Am I like "the disciples who understand nothing, who fell asleep while the Lord was suffering?" Or "am I like Pilate? When I see that the situation is difficult, do I wash my hands and dodge my responsibility, allowing people to be condemned or condemning them myself?" Or "am I like those fearless women, and like the mother of Jesus, who were there and who suffered in silence?"

Concluding his remarks, Pope Francis invited people throughout the days leading to Easter to ask: "Where is my heart?" Which person in the story of the Lord's passion "am I like?"

FOOT WASHING

Pope Francis has the custom, dating back to his time as archbishop of Buenos Aires, Argentina, of celebrating the Holy Thursday evening Mass of the Lord's Supper in a prison, hospital, shelter or other place

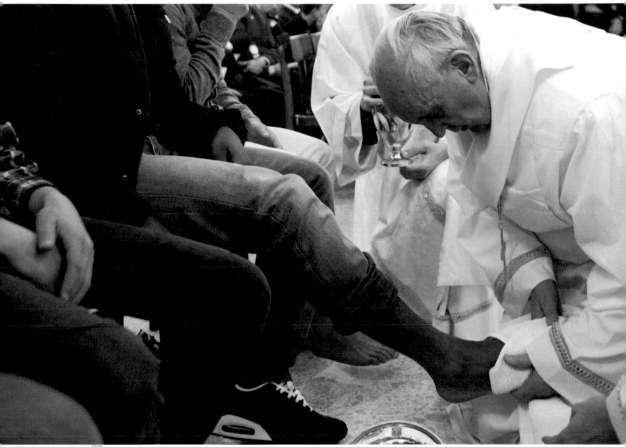

CASAL DEL MARMO JUVENILE DETENTION CENTER, ROME, MARCH 28, 2013

with people often thought to be living on the margins of society. Continuing that tradition as pope, he celebrated the evening Mass in 2013 at a juvenile detention facility and in 2014 at a rehabilitation center for people with physical or emotional disabilities.

The foot-washing ritual that is part of the Holy Thursday Mass recalls Jesus' washing of his disciples' feet at the Last Supper. At the juvenile detention center where he celebrated this Mass in 2013, Pope Francis asked the young people to think of the foot washing as "a caress of Jesus, which Jesus gives because this is the real reason Jesus came: to serve, to help us." The following year, at the rehabilitation center, the pope explained that by washing his disciples' feet, Jesus communicated the message that he, who was God, became a servant and that those who follow him must serve others as well.

"That is why the church on this day that commemorates the Last Supper, when Jesus instituted the Eucharist, also repeats this gesture of washing feet, which reminds us that we must serve one another," Pope Francis told the rehabilitation center's residents and staff. Jesus "took this path for love," and "you too must love one another and be servants, in love," said the pope. "This is the legacy Jesus leaves us."

COLOSSEUM, ROME, APRIL 18, 2014

COLOSSEUM, ROME, APRIL 18, 2014

St. Peter's Square, April 20, 2014

ONE AMONG THE DEAD?

"[WE HAVE]
A TRUE AND DEEP
JOY FOUNDED
ON THE CERTAINTY
THAT THE RISEN
CHRIST SHALL
NEVER DIE AGAIN;
RATHER, HE IS ALIVE
AND AT WORK
IN THE CHURCH
AND IN THE WORLD."

(POPE FRANCIS, APRIL 23, 2014)

"J esus is the everlasting 'today' of God," Pope Francis proclaimed on his first Easter as pope. For the women who found the tomb of Jesus empty when they went the first Easter to anoint his body, nothing remained the same, the pope said. Nothing remains the same "in our own lives" either, because Jesus "is alive! He does not simply return to life; rather, he is life itself."

A year later, the Monday after Easter 2014, Pope Francis suggested to visitors in St. Peter's Square that they rejoice all week "as though it were one single day." This is a time in the liturgical year to "relive the disciples' state of mind over the news" the women brought from the tomb: "Jesus is risen! We have seen him!"

So great is Easter that the church rejoices all the way to Pentecost, 50 days later. "Let us allow the joyous wonder of Easter Sunday to shine

St. Peter's Square, March 31, 2013

forth in our thoughts, glances, behavior, gestures and words," Pope Francis exhorted the crowd that Easter Monday. Experiencing the resurrection's joy enables us, he said, to carry "a 'ray' of the light of the Risen One" to people who are happy, "making them more beautiful by preserving them from selfishness," and to people who suffer, "bringing serenity and hope."

Pope Francis returned to the theme of joy several days later during an early morning Mass in the chapel of his Vatican residence. Christians cannot live as if life were "a nonstop funeral," he insisted, although sometimes "we are afraid of being close to Jesus because this gives us joy." Coining the phrase "bat Christians," the pope explained that some people fear basking in Christ's light and joy, preferring to dwell like bats in dark caves, frightened to believe Christ is at their side. "We ask the Lord for the grace not to be afraid of joy," he prayed.

ST. PETER'S BASILICA, MARCH 30, 2013

During the 2014 Easter season, Pope Francis led participants at a morning Mass deeper into what it means for individuals and Christian communities to live as if they really believe Jesus rose from the dead. Drawing upon the Acts of the Apostles' description of the earliest Christian community (4:32-35), he noted how faith in the risen Lord leads to

St. Peter's Basilica, April 19, 2014

communities that are united, share joy with others and help the poor. Catholics and their parishes, he said, must "give witness that Jesus is alive among us."

A checklist appeared in that homily. Pope Francis, a Jesuit, often offers checklists for reviewing our response to God's grace. This is his adaptation of the *Examen*, which St. Ignatius of Loyola, the Jesuits' founder, encouraged his men to perform at midday and bedtime. The pope suggested that people ask: "Is my community at peace and in harmony or is it divided? Does my community give witness to Jesus Christ; does it know Christ is risen? Or does it just know this intellectually but not do anything about it, not proclaim it? Does my community take care of the poor? Is it a poor community," relying on God, not money or power?

Pope Francis knows how to use questions to challenge people. He did this at the 2013 Easter Vigil and his general audience the Wednesday after Easter in 2014, asking, "Why do you seek the living One among the dead?" Angels posed this very question to the women who went to Jesus' tomb to anoint his body (Lk 24:5).

"Daily problems and worries can wrap us up in ourselves, in sadness and bitterness, and that is where death is," Pope Francis cautioned. But,

St. Peter's Basilica, June 8, 2014

he exclaimed: "That is not the place to look for the One who is alive!" During the vigil Mass, at which he baptized, confirmed and gave first Communion to four young men, he prayed that, like the newly baptized, all Christians would allow the risen Jesus into their lives and become

73

open "to the newness that transforms, to the beautiful surprises of God."

Do not go to "tombs that promise something but in the end give nothing," Pope Francis counseled visitors and pilgrims in Rome the Wednesday after Easter 2014. People often try to seek life among things "that cannot give life, among things that exist today and are gone tomorrow" like worldly power, money and success. But these are dead ends, he warned. Pope Francis challenged his listeners directly, asking: "Why do you seek the living One among the dead, you who withdraw into your-

St. Peter's Square, April 20, 2014

self after a failure and you who no longer have the strength to pray? Why do you seek the living One among the dead, you who feel alone, abandoned by friends and perhaps also by God?" Horizons of hope and joy open, the pope said, when we repeat and remind each other that Jesus "is alive" and is "with us!"

The search for the living God is essential to the Christian journey, and Pope Francis continually urges people to pursue it. His words during the 2014 Easter Vigil explored what it meant when the disciples

were told – first by an angel, then by the risen Lord – to return to Galilee where they first met Jesus. For today's Christians, returning to Galilee "means reviving the memory of that moment when his eyes met mine, the moment when he made me realize he loved me." But the pope made clear that returning to Galilee is not about nostalgia or backtracking. It is about remembering all Jesus did in your life and rereading your experiences – happy or painful – in light of his death and resurrection. This type of memory helps get us back on track when we are distracted from our journey; it yields a fresh perspective on our sufferings.

A return to Galilee "ignites a humble joy" that sorrow and distress will not extinguish, said Pope Francis. And we return "to our first love in order to receive the fire that Jesus kindled in the world and bring that fire to all people."

At the very start of the Easter season, then, Pope Francis raised a question that all can ask: "Where is my Galilee? Do I remember it?" He added, "There the Lord awaits you."

THE ASCENSION

As the Easter season advances closer to its conclusion, Christians celebrate the feast of the Ascension of the Lord. "Jesus' earthly life culminated with the Ascension, when he passed from this world to the Father and was raised to sit on his right," Pope Francis noted during a 2013 Wednesday general audience. Yet, "the Ascension does not point to Jesus' absence," he said. It "tells us he is alive in our midst in a new way."

When Jesus went up to Jerusalem for the last time, he knew the path leading him to the glory of the Father would pass "through the cross, through obedience to the divine plan of love for humankind," Pope Francis remarked. The love that led Jesus to give his life for all continues now; seated at the Father's right hand, he is our advocate. "When someone is summoned by a judge or is involved in legal proceedings, the first thing he does is to seek a lawyer to defend him," said the pope. "We have One who always defends us," defends us from the "snares of the devil" and "from ourselves and our sins!" The Ascension assures us, too, of the "consoling reality" that "in Christ, true God and true man, our humanity was taken to God. Christ opened the path to us."

St. Peter's Basilica, April 19, 2014

76

PENTECOST

After 50 days of joy, the feast of Pentecost concludes the Easter season. Now "the church relives the outpouring of the Spirit upon Mary and the apostles gathered in prayer in the Upper Room," Pope Francis explained shortly before Pentecost 2013. He described the weeks of Easter Time as the season "par excellence" of "the Holy Spirit given 'without measure' (cf. Jn 3:34)." When he celebrated this feast with

members of Catholic movements in 2013, Pope Francis called the Pentecost liturgy "a great prayer that the church in union with Jesus raises up to the Father, asking him to renew the outpouring of the Holy Spirit."

Pentecost celebrates the gifts of the Holy Spirit, which enable the Lord's disciples to preach the Gospel to the ends of the earth. On the first Pentecost of his pontificate, Pope Francis focused on the newness the Holy Spirit brings, the harmony the Spirit's

ST. PETER'S SQUARE, APRIL 20, 2014

gifts should create in a community and how the Spirit prompts Christians to share the Good News with others. The Holy Spirit, he stressed, is not trying to relieve our boredom but to show a new way to "true joy, true serenity." Pope Francis asked: "Are we open to 'God's surprises'? Or are we closed and fearful before the newness of the Holy Spirit?"

The Spirit bestows a variety of gifts among the church's members, but this need not conflict with their harmony because "the Holy Spirit is the Spirit of unity," Pope Francis observed. It is the Spirit, he said, who

"can awaken diversity, plurality and multiplicity, while at the same time building unity."

Finally, Pope Francis characterized the Holy Spirit as "the soul of mission," who impels us to open the doors of the church "and go forth to proclaim and bear witness to the good news of the Gospel, to communicate the joy of faith."

ST. PETER'S SQUARE, OCT. 9, 2013

Into God's Promise

"No one
is a Christian
by pure accident.
No one.
You are called,
you and you
and you."

(Pope **FRANCIS**, June 25, 2013)

od calls each person "by name and with a promise: 'Go out. I am with you. I walk beside you,'" Pope Francis told those who joined him for an early morning Mass in the chapel at his residence June 25, 2013. God calls us personally, "one by one," just as he called the patriarch Abraham in the Book of Genesis. God spoke to Abraham, "gave him a promise and invited him to come out of his land," the pope pointed out. Trusting God, Abraham "departed his land" and journeyed "toward this promise." As was true of Abraham, the pope added, a promise accompanies God's call today, and it "keeps us going."

Following Jesus "is a call of love and friendship, a call to become a child of God." Moreover, it is a call "to become fruitful in transmitting this call to others," Pope Francis said. Of course, "there are difficult

CASSANO ALL'JONIO, ITALY, **JUNE 21, 2014**

times," and "Jesus had many of his own." Yet, always there is the confidence that "the Lord has called me" and "has promised me."

For Pope Francis, the 33 or 34 weeks of Ordinary Time — first, between the January feast of the Baptism of the Lord and Ash Wednesday; then between Pentecost and the start of Advent — offer lessons in discipleship. The Scripture readings during these many weeks share details of Jesus' public preaching and healing, recount his parables and miracles, and show, in the experience of the apostles, how hard it can be to understand Jesus and what a blessing it is to walk alongside him. During Ordinary Time the liturgy invites God's people to grow in the life of Christ and participate more fully in the community of believers.

"Jesus does not want to act alone; he came to bring the love of God into the world, and he wants to spread it in the style of communion, in the style of brotherhood," Pope Francis told a crowd gathered in St. Pe-

St. Peter's Square, June 12, 2014

ter's Square early in July 2013. At the beginning of his public ministry, Jesus "forms a community of disciples, which is a missionary community."

Pope Francis also accented the church's community life on the feast of Corpus Christi – the feast of the Body and Blood of the Lord – that

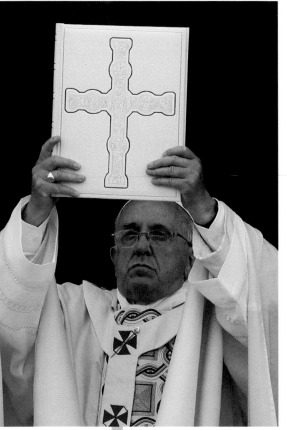

year, calling the Eucharist "the sacrament of communion that brings us out of individualism so that we may follow [the Lord] together." The pope challenged believers to ask: "How do I live the Eucharist? Do I live it anonymously or as a moment of true communion with the Lord and also with all the brothers and sisters who share this same banquet?".

So for Pope Francis, placing Christ at the center of life means having a personal relationship with him, but also a relationship with his body, the church. During a general audience talk in May 2013, he mentioned an objection he hears: "Christ yes, the church no." But this attitude makes little sense, he said, because "it is the church herself that brings Christ to us and brings us to God." He acknowledged

BASILICA OF ST. JOHN LATERAN, ROME, JUNE 19, 2014

that the church "has human aspects. In those who make up the church, pastors and faithful, there are shortcomings, imperfections and sins." Yet, "the church is the great family of God's children," he said. Pray, he urged, "that our communities, the whole church, be increasingly true families that live and bring the warmth of God."

PENTECOST TO ADVENT

The longest stretch of Ordinary Time runs between Pentecost and the start of Advent, and begins with the feast of the Holy Trinity. On the heels of Jesus' resurrection at Easter and the outpouring of the Holy

WESTERN WALL, JERUSALEM, MAY 26, 2014

Spirit on Pentecost, the Bible readings of Ordinary Time urge Catholics to contemplate the reality and the relationship of God the Father, Son and Holy Spirit.

"God is not something vague, our God is not a God 'spray,' he is tangible; he is not abstract but has a name: 'God is love,'" Pope Francis stated on the feast of the Holy Trinity in 2013. Easter and Pentecost renew awareness that Jesus' love "is not a sentimental, emotional kind of love, but the love of the Father, who is the origin of all life, the love of the Son, who dies on the cross and is raised, the love of the Spirit, who renews human beings and the world." To think of God as love "does us so much good," said the pope. "It teaches us to love, to give ourselves to others as Jesus gave himself to us and walks with us."

Soon after Trinity Sunday, Catholics celebrate the feast of the Body and Blood of Christ. In Rome and many other places around the world, the feast includes a Corpus Christi procession, with people of faith accompanying the Blessed Sacrament through city streets. For Pope Francis the procession celebrates Christ's presence in the Eucharist, while also serving as a concrete reminder that all Jesus' disciples are called to follow him along society's highways and byways.

Jesus "gives himself to us in the Eucharist, shares in our journey, indeed he makes himself

St. Peter's Square, Nov. 20, 2013

food, the true food that sustains our life, including at moments when the road becomes hard going," Pope Francis affirmed in a 2013 Corpus Christi homily. "In the Eucharist the Lord makes us walk on his road, that of service, of sharing, of giving." After speaking of Jesus' multiplication of five loaves and two fish to feed 5,000 hungry people (Lk 9:12-17), Pope Francis insisted that "in the church, but also in society, a key word we must not fear is *solidarity*, that is, the ability to make what we have, our humble capacities, available to God, for only in sharing, in giving, will our life be fruitful." And when we share the little we have, God's power "comes down into our poverty to transform it."

Pope Francis insists on the importance of church members modeling their relationships on those of the earliest Christians, who according to the Acts of the Apostles were of "one mind and one heart" (4:32). However, the devil delights in division and rancor in parishes, dioceses and the church at large, the pope cautions.

In the pope's eyes — he says this in many homilies — gossip is one of the devil's favorite tools for breaking down relationships. In June 2013 he told a small congregation in the chapel at his residence that one of the keys to Christian life is learning to "be more attentive to our tongues and what we say about others." If we harbor "bad feelings" toward others in the community, "something is not working and we must convert," he concluded. He recommended asking the Lord for the grace "to watch what we say about others." This is "a small penance," he added, but "it bears a lot of fruit."

Some people are surprised how often Pope Francis refers to himself as a sinner, but he is convinced the way to grow in holiness and compassion is to recognize our faults and acknowledge the mercy shown by God in our own lives. If we focus exclusively on our own record of accomplishments as Christians, he said at a morning Mass, "we cannot proclaim Jesus Christ as Savior." Humility is necessary for Christians, the pope believes, but it must be "real" and lead one to confess, "I am a sinner for this, for this, for this."

COPACABANA BEACH, RIO DE JANEIRO, BRAZIL, JULY 25, 2013

Self-reflection is an important part of the Christian life, and it is good for every Christian to ponder Jesus' question to his disciples in Luke 9:20: "Who do you say that I am?" Pope Francis highlighted that question when he celebrated Mass in June 2013 with about 40 archbishops serving as Vatican ambassadors around the world. "Who am I for you?" The question asks us that, the pope indicated. Notably, it is "asked by a living person, and we have to respond from the heart." Like the apostle Peter, we must be honest in our response because, after all, Jesus knows all things. "Never be ashamed, don't hide your sins," because Jesus "loves us very much when we see ourselves as sinners."

Getting to know Jesus more fully is essential in Christian life, but "one cannot know Jesus without getting involved with him," Pope Francis told participants in a September 2013 Mass. You cannot know Jesus by sitting "in first class" or in a library, he said. "To know him you must

BASILICA OF ST. JOHN LATERAN, ROME, JUNE 19, 2014

dialogue with him, speak with him in prayer, on your knees," and follow him, just as the disciples did.

Prayer and action are two essentials of Christian life, and one is not opposed to the other, Pope Francis commented in July 2013 remarks at a Sunday Angelus. He focused on the Gospel story of Martha and Mary, which recounts one sister, Mary, sitting at the feet of Jesus and listening to him, while her sister Martha is "burdened with much serving" (Lk 10:38-42). But, said the pope, these biblical women do not represent "contradictory attitudes: listening to the word of the Lord, contemplation; and practical service to our neighbor." In fact, "prayer that does not lead you to practical action for your brother or sister — the poor, the sick, those in need of help, those in difficulty — is sterile and incomplete prayer." Yet, service cannot be so focused on doing and building that "we forget the centrality of Christ. When time is not set aside for di-

DOMUS SANCTAE MARTHAE, VATICAN, OCT. 24, 2013

alogue with him in prayer, we risk serving ourselves and not God present in our needy brother and sister," the pope continued.

"Faith is a walk with Jesus. Remember this always: Faith is walking with Jesus, and it is a walk that lasts a lifetime. At the end there shall be the definitive encounter," Pope Francis said in November 2013 when he met with a group of men and women who were entering the catechumenate, their formal preparation for baptism. He examined three essential steps in the life of faith awaiting them: hearing someone proclaim Jesus; encountering Jesus; then walking with him. "Certainly, at some moments on the journey we feel tired and confused, but faith gives us the certainty of Jesus' constant presence in every situation, even the most painful," the pope said. He counseled the catechumens that whenever a person "ceases to thirst for the living God, faith is in danger of becoming a habit, it risks being extinguished, like a fire that is not fed."

As the church's liturgical year advances toward its conclusion, the Scripture readings at Masses speak more often of the final judgment and eternal life. Celebrating the feast of Christ the King in 2013, Ordinary Time's final Sunday, Pope Francis explained to crowds gathered for a Mass in St. Peter's Square that the journey of faith "has as its ultimate end our full encounter with God." All along the journey, "the Holy Spirit purifies us, lifts us up and sanctifies us so that we may enter into the happiness for which our hearts long."

Amman, Jordan, May 24, 2014

In speaking of Christ as king, Christians recognize him as the Lord of history, the center of creation and a clear sign of God's mercy and reconciliation, Pope Francis declared. It gives us hope, moreover, to realize that "God's grace is always greater than the prayer which sought it." For, said the pope, the Lord is "so generous" that "he always gives more" than we ask of him.

Basilica of St. Mary Major, Rome, May 30, 2013

Verano cemetery, Rome, **Nov. 1, 2013**

THE GREAT WORKS OF GOD

"WHENEVER
WE LOOK TO MARY,
WE COME TO BELIEVE
ONCE AGAIN
IN THE REVOLUTIONARY
NATURE OF LOVE
AND TENDERNESS.
IN HER WE SEE
THAT HUMILITY
AND TENDERNESS
ARE NOT VIRTUES
OF THE WEAK BUT
OF THE STRONG."

(POPE FRANCIS, "THE JOY OF THE GOSPEL")

Whenever Pope Francis passes a statue or icon of the Virgin Mary he kisses it or allows his hand to rest tenderly upon it. His devotion to Mary is tangible. He traveled early in the morning the day after his election to Rome's Basilica of St. Mary Major. There he entrusted his papacy and Rome, his new diocese, to Mary. In a basilica chapel he prayed before the "Salvation of the Roman People," an ancient icon of Mary and the child Jesus.

Mary is both mother and model for Pope Francis. "It is from Mary that the church learns true discipleship," the pope said in Brazil during the 2013 World Youth Day. Repeatedly, he calls attention not only to Mary's humble origins but to her complete trust in God, even though the divine plan for her life sounded so extraordinary and would bring such pain along with joy.

PAPAL FLIGHT TO BRAZIL, JULY 22, 2013

Deep devotion to Mary characterizes the spirituality of all modern popes. A large letter *M* on St. John Paul II's coat of arms signified how essential she was to his identity as a Christian, bishop and pope.

The Catholic Church's liturgical calendar is filled with Marian feasts, including three holy days of obligation: the Jan. 1 solemnity of Mary, Mother of God; the Aug. 15 feast of the Assumption; and the Dec. 8 feast of the Immaculate Conception. During his pontificate's first year, Pope Francis also marked the May 8 feast of Our Lady of Lujan, patroness of his native Argentina, and the Dec. 12 feast of Our Lady of Guadalupe. He celebrated Masses at Brazil's Shrine of Our Lady of Aparecida and Italy's Shrine of Our Lady of Bonaria. When he makes a public prayer request — for peace in a world trouble spot, for unemployed workers, for frazzled parents — he almost always invites the crowd to pray a Hail Mary with him.

BASILICA OF ST. MARY MAJOR, ROME, **MAY 4, 2013**

ST. PETER'S SQUARE, OCT. 13, 2013

98

"Let us invoke Mary's intercession. May she help us to be open to God's surprises," Pope Francis urged in an October 2013 homily delivered in St. Peter's Square. Mary's experience of the surprises of God resembles our experience, the pope suggested. For "it is precisely in poverty, in weakness and in humility that he reveals himself and grants us his love, which saves us, heals us and gives us strength. He asks us only to obey his word and to trust him."

Mary did not hide her surprise when the Angel Gabriel first revealed that she would bear God's Son, Pope Francis noted. Hers was the astonishment of realizing that God chose her, "a simple maid of Nazareth — not someone who lived in a palace amid power and riches or one who had done extraordinary things." God chose someone open to him, someone who "put her trust in him, even

SHRINE OF OUR LADY OF APARECIDA, BRAZIL, JULY 24, 2013

without understanding everything." The pope recommended that people ask themselves: "Do I let myself be surprised by God, as Mary was, or do I remain caught up in my own safety zone …, taking refuge in my own projects and plans? Do I truly let God into my life?"

Jan. 1 is the day each year when the church celebrates not only the feast of Mary, Mother of God, but the World Day of Peace, established in 1967 by Pope Paul VI. "Two roads intersect today," Pope Francis noted on his first New Year's Day as pope. Yet the day of peace fits well with this feast of Mary because true peace is a gift of the Holy Spirit, he observed. The Spirit "is the power of life which made the womb of the Virgin Mary fruitful, and it is the same power which inspires the efforts and work of all builders of peace."

Entrusting to Mary "the cry for peace of peoples who are oppressed by war and violence," Pope Francis prayerfully pleaded that "the courage of dialogue and reconciliation might prevail over temptations of revenge, tyranny and corruption."

Pope Francis told worshipers in St. Peter's Basilica earlier that day that *Mother of God* is "the first and most important title of Our Lady. It refers to a quality, a role that the faith of the Christian people ... understood from the beginning." Pointing to the Gospel of John (19:27), the pope recalled that Jesus, dying on the cross, gave his mother to all believers, saying, "Behold your mother."

Thus, "the 'woman' became our mother when she lost her divine Son. Her sorrowing heart was enlarged to make room for all men and women – all, whether good or bad – and she loves them as she loved Jesus," Pope Francis continued. Therefore, "to her let us entrust our journey of faith, the desires of our heart, our needs

and the needs of the whole world, especially of those who hunger and thirst for justice and peace, and for God."

On the Aug. 15 feast of the Assumption of Mary, the church turns its attention to the end of her earthly life when she was taken up, body and soul, to heaven. Mary "entered, once and for all, into heavenly glory," the pope affirmed during a 2013 Mass on this feast day at Castel Gandolfo, the papal summer residence. Nonetheless, he stressed, Mary "walks with us always." Entering heavenly glory "does not mean she is distant or detached from us; rather, Mary accompanies us, struggles with us."

To the small congregation packed into the tiny parish church in Castel Gandolfo and to the thousands watching from the town square outside, Pope Francis explained that even as Mary "lived her Son's passion to the depths of her soul," she was filled with hope. "Hope is the virtue of

101

those who, experiencing conflict – the struggle between life and death, good and evil – believe in the resurrection of Christ, in the victory of love," he said.

Mary's *Magnificat* (Lk 1:46-55), her canticle of praise and trust in God, is for Pope Francis "the song of hope." It is the song of "many

saints — men and women, some famous and very many others unknown to us but known to God: moms, dads, catechists, missionaries, priests, sisters, young people, even children and grandparents," he said. It is the song of those who face "the struggle of life while carrying within their hearts the hope of the little and the humble."

Lourdes Grotto, Vatican Gardens, May 31, 2014

For Mary and for us, saying yes to God is essential in the journey of faith, Pope Francis pointed out in brief remarks after the Castel Gandolfo Mass. "Mary's journey to heaven began with the yes spoken in Nazareth in response to the heavenly messenger's announcement to her of God's will," the pope said. "And in reality it is exactly like this: Every yes to God is a step toward heaven, toward eternal life. Because this is what the Lord wants: that all his children may have life in abundance! God wants us all with him, in his house!"

THE IMMACULATE CONCEPTION

The popes for more than 60 years have marked the Dec. 8 feast of Mary's Immaculate Conception by traveling the short distance from Vatican City to a square near the famed Spanish Steps in the center of Rome. They place flowers at the foot of a statue of Mary originally blessed by Pope Pius IX in 1857, three years after he defined the dogma that God preserved Mary from original sin from the moment of her conception.

Instead of delivering a speech when he arrived at the Spanish Steps on the first Dec. 8 of his pontificate, Pope Francis recited a prayer to Mary "all beautiful" that included this verse:

In you there is no sin.

Awaken in all of us a renewed desire for holiness:

SPANISH STEPS, ROME, DEC. 8, 2013

May the splendor of truth shine forth in our words,

the song of charity resound in our works,

purity and chastity abide in our hearts and bodies,

and the full beauty of the Gospel be evident in our lives.

ST. PETER'S SQUARE, APRIL 20, 2014

At the Vatican earlier in the day, Pope Francis told those who gathered for the recitation of the Angelus that we hail Mary as the one "full of grace" because "this is how God saw her from the first moment of his loving design." God chose Mary, "a girl from Nazareth, a small town in Galilee, on the outskirts of the Roman Empire and the outskirts of Israel as well," to be the mother of his Son. "In view of this motherhood, Mary was preserved from original sin, from that fracture in communion with

God, with others and with creation that deeply wounds every human being," the pope said. "This fracture was healed in advance in the mother of the One who came to free us from the slavery of sin." The Immaculate Virgin Mary "is the fruit of God's love that saves the world," Pope Francis proclaimed.

He entreated his listeners to allow Mary to watch over them in order to "learn how to be more humble and also more courageous in following the Word of God." In "contemplating our beautiful Immaculate Mother," he said, "let us also recognize our truest destiny, our deepest vocation: to be loved, to be transformed by love, to be transformed by the beauty of God."

WESTERN WALL, JERUSALEM, MAY 26, 2014

GOD FORGIVES

"GOD NEVER TIRES
OF FORGIVING US;
WE ARE THE ONES
WHO TIRE OF SEEKING
HIS MERCY.
CHRIST, WHO TOLD US
TO FORGIVE
ONE ANOTHER
'SEVENTY TIMES
SEVEN,' . . .
HAS FORGIVEN US
SEVENTY
TIMES SEVEN."

(POPE FRANCIS, "THE JOY OF THE GOSPEL")

"If you want to know the tenderness of a father, try turning to God. Try it, and then tell me how it went," Pope Francis confidently suggested to participants in a March 2014 early morning Mass. God's call to *convert*, to change our lives, is strong and demanding, the pope stated. Yet, inside the word *convert* we encounter mercy; we encounter "the loving yearning of God" calling: "Come back. Come back. It is time to come back home."

While the parable of the prodigal son from the Gospel of Luke (15:11-32) is read at Sunday Masses only twice every three years, Pope Francis mentions it again and again throughout the liturgical year. The parable of the shepherd who goes in search of his lost sheep (Mt 18:12-14 and Lk 15:3-7) is another of the pope's favorite Bible stories. Taken together, these parables show that in every season God the Father watches over all his children, not just awaiting them but going in search

ST. GREGORY THE GREAT PARISH, ROME, APRIL 6, 2014

of them. Indeed, God's merciful first reaction when the wayward return home is to throw a party.

"God's face is the face of a merciful father who is always patient," the pope told the crowds in St. Peter's Square for his first Sunday Angelus address, just four days after his March 2013 election. God "waits for us, he does not tire of forgiving us if we are able to return to him with a contrite heart." The problem, the pope commented, is that "we do not want to ask or we grow weary of asking for forgiveness." He prayed not only that people would accept God's mercy but would "learn to be merciful" to others as well.

One day in Lent 2014, when the first reading for Mass, Hosea 14:2-10, began with a call to Israel to return to God, Pope Francis encouraged those at his morning Mass to contemplate "the beautiful icon of the father and the prodigal son." When the returning son was still far off, his father

nonetheless noticed him coming because he "went out on the terrace every day to watch for him," the pope pointed out. On the way home, the son rehearsed in his head a whole speech about how undeserving of forgiveness he was. But when he finally arrives, "the father doesn't let him speak." He embraces his son and calls the servants to prepare a feast.

RIO DE JANEIRO, BRAZIL, JULY 25, 2013

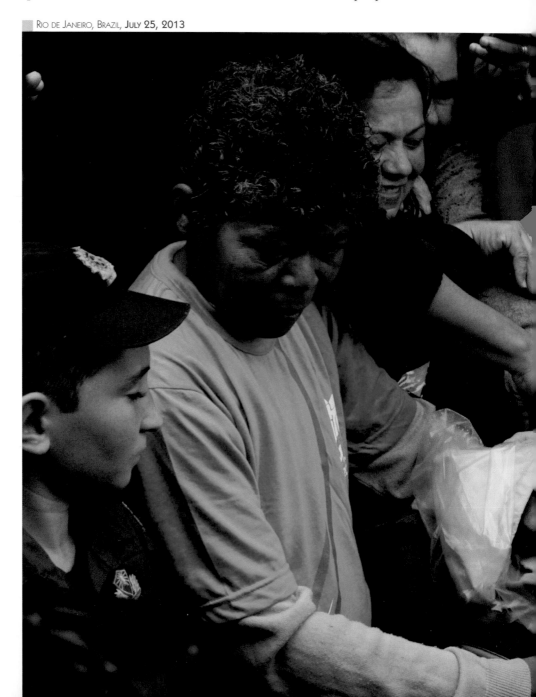

The Bible tells the story of God waiting for people to come back to him, of God forgiving them and celebrating their return, said the pope. "The life of every person, of every man and woman, who has the courage to draw near to the Lord, will end with the joy of God's celebration."

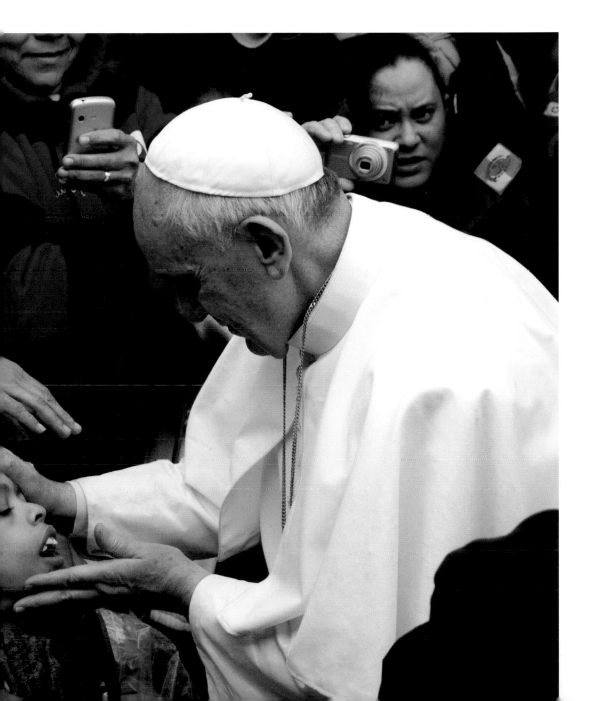

The fact that God is so merciful does not mean our sins are not sins, Pope Francis emphasized during another early morning Mass; but "mercy is the way God forgives," and his forgiveness removes sins. The pope explained: "It is like the sky. If we look at the [night] sky, there are many stars, but when the sun comes up in the morning, with all its light, you don't see the stars anymore." In the light of God's mercy, our sins no longer are visible.

God's pardon comes not "with a decree, but with a caress," Pope Francis continued. He pointed to the Gospel story of the woman caught in adultery. Jesus does not humiliate her, the pope observed. "He doesn't say: 'What have you done? When did you do it? How did you do it?" He rather says, "Go and sin no more." The pope exclaimed: "God's mercy is great, Jesus' mercy is great!"

While human justice aims to give people exactly what they deserve, Pope Francis insists that God's justice goes beyond such simple math. God is being just to himself in

ST. PETER'S SQUARE, SEPT. 7, 2013

forgiving sins because God is in the business of forgiving and trying to bring us all to eternal life.

God cannot stand to lose one of his children, Pope Francis said during a November 2013 Mass in his residence's chapel. Moreover, God has "a kind of weakness of love for those who are farthest off, who are lost, and he goes out in search of them." But God's "job" is not simply to find the lost. God brings them back and restores them to their rightful place in the flock. Pope Francis said, "The joy of God is not the death of a sinner, but his life." So even if someone says, "But I'm a sinner – I've done this, this and this," God will respond, "'I love you anyway, and I'll go out to find you, and I'll bring you home.' This is our Father. He always comes searching for us."

Pope Francis wants people to recognize the sacrament of reconciliation as an opportunity to experience God's tenderness. The confessional is "not a torture chamber," nor is the priest there to berate penitents, he promised during a morning Mass in April 2013. In meetings with priests he underscores the importance of mirroring God's mercy in this sacrament. Speaking with priests of the Rome Diocese at the beginning of Lent 2014, Pope Francis shared the story of a confessor in Argentina who used to fear he was too quick to grant absolution. The priest would enter the chapel to pray about this before the tabernacle and would say, "Forgive me, Lord, if I pardon too much, but I'm just following your example."

The pope repeated that story after Easter 2014 when he met privately with deacons he was about to ordain to the priesthood. Later, at their ordination Mass May 11, he reminded them of the story and said: "For the love of Jesus Christ, never tire of being merciful. Please. Be as forgiving as the Lord, who came not to condemn but to forgive. Have mercy, a lot of it!" Continuing, Pope Francis confessed it grieves him when he hears people say that "they don't go to confession anymore be-

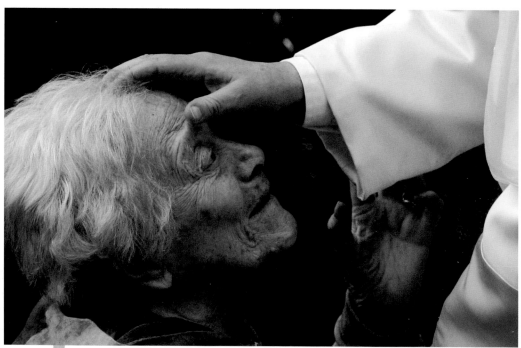

PAUL VI AUDIENCE HALL, VATICAN, MARCH 29, 2014

SHRINE OF OUR LADY OF BONARIA, CAGLIARI, ITALY, **SEPT. 22, 2013**

cause they were scolded, yelled at. They felt like the doors of the church were being slammed shut in their faces." He pleaded, "Please, don't do that. Mercy. Mercy!"

Responding to a reporter's question during an in-flight press conference while returning to Rome from the July 2013 World Youth Day in Rio de Janeiro, Brazil, Pope Francis explained that in mentioning mercy frequently he is highlighting an often-overlooked but sorely needed aspect of church teaching. "This is the time for mercy," he said. "The church is mother and must follow the path of mercy and find mercy for everyone."

Less than a month after his election, Pope Francis celebrated Mass in Rome's Basilica of St. John Lateran. It was the Sunday after Easter, the day St. John Paul II decreed would be celebrated as Divine Mercy Sunday for the worldwide church. Pope Francis told worshipers that whenever we allow ourselves to be loved by God "and to encounter his mercy in the sacraments," we are certain to "feel his wonderful tenderness, we will feel his embrace, and we too will become more capable of mercy, patience, forgiveness and love."

VATICAN GARDENS, JUNE 8, 2014

FROM MERCY TO PEACE

When he solemnly offered his blessing to the church and the world (*urbi et orbi*) on the first Easter of his pontificate, Pope Francis asked people everywhere to become "agents" of God's mercy. It "can make even the driest land become a garden, can restore life to dry bones," the pope

proclaimed. Therefore, "we ask the risen Jesus, who turns death into life, to change hatred into love, vengeance into forgiveness, war into peace."

In their Easter messages the popes traditionally pray for specific countries or regions at war, as well as for peace around the globe. The crowds that gathered in St. Peter's Square on Easter 2013 heard Pope Francis plead for an end to violence in many places, and they heard him offer an urgent invitation "to everyone" that said:

"Let us be renewed by God's mercy, let us be loved by Jesus, let us enable the power of his love to transform our lives too; and let us become agents of this mercy, channels through which God can water the earth, protect all creation and make justice and peace flourish."

ACKNOWLEDGMENTS

This book and its content reflect the ideas, enthusiasm and hard work of many talented and dedicated people at Catholic News Service, the Communications Department of the U.S. Conference of Catholic Bishops and the Libreria Editrice Vaticana.

The author and photographer would like to give special thanks to David Gibson, retired founding editor of CNS Origins Documentary Service and longtime editor of its Faith Alive! religious education supplement. Gibson edited this book with wisdom, passion for accuracy and clarity, and endless patient collaboration.

This project was the brainchild of CNS Rome Bureau Chief Francis X. Rocca and Anthony J. Spence, editor in chief of CNS, who demonstrated confidence and flexibility throughout its production. Carol Glatz, CNS Vatican correspondent, always good natured, clocked extra hours covering the daily Vatican news flow as the author worked on the text, but also was invaluable in identifying the essential gems of wisdom from Pope Francis' morning Mass homilies. Mary Esslinger, with her wealth of knowledge and experience, made significant improvements to the text. Salesian Father Giuseppe Costa, director of LEV, was a driving force behind the project and remarkably adept at innocently asking, "How's it going?" and making it clear at the same time that he expected to see the project completed soon.

Cindy Wooden also thanks the talented and hardworking Paul Haring for his beautiful photographs, his suggestions, critiques and encouragement. Cindy also would like to acknowledge her parents, now deceased, especially her mother who introduced her to the faith with a combination of serious commitment, joy and down-to-earth wisdom often remarkably similar to that of Pope Francis.

Photographer Paul Haring would like to thank his Italian colleagues, whose kindness and camaraderie have made light the long hours photographing the pope and the Vatican. He is also grateful to Cindy Wooden who has always generously and enthusiastically shared her extensive knowledge of the papacy and the Vatican. He could not have completed the project without the support of his wife, Ann, who provided advice and encouragement and more than a few late night dinners.

Printed in Italy